MW01124480

Young Black
Millionairess™

How to Start a Million-Dollar Business

Get to the Point Edition™
Volume 1/2

Taysha **Valez**

Note: This book is the introduction to Volume 1,
the full-length, all-detail version, *Young Black Millionairess*™:
How to Start a Million-Dollar Business,
which will be available at the end of the year.

Cover photo	*www.mediagenerators.net*
	Jennifer Wasson
Cover design	*Jennifer Wasson*
Copyeditor	*Jennifer Wasson*

Copyright © 2005, H.Couture Publishing. All rights reserved. No part of this work may be reproduced in any form, or by any means, without the permission of the publisher. Exceptions are made for brief excerpts to be used in published reviews.

This publication is designed to provide general information regarding the subject matter covered. However, laws and practices often vary from state to state and are subject to change. The author has taken reasonable precautions in the preparation of this book and believes the facts presented in the book are accurate as of the date it was written. However, neither the author nor the publisher assume any responsibility for any errors or omissions. The author and publisher specifically disclaim any liability resulting from the use or application of the information contained in this book. The information is not intended to serve as legal and professional advice related to individual situations.

H.Couture Publishing
Division of H.Couture Beauty L.L.C.

Taysha Valez CEO/President

ISBN: 0-9767680-5-4

"*Do not quote without prior permission from the publisher.*"
"For content only"

The end interludes are bonus tracks (thank you)

Printed in the United States of America

Portions of the proceeds from this book will go to www.beautywaterorg.com, a nonprofit organization that provides grants to small businesses, scholarships, low-cost and often free business education, as well as grants to cover treatment cost for those living with HIV/AIDS and breast cancer.

Contents

Acknowledgments

People who made this book and H.Couture possible

Lisa Pellegrene
President/CEO of Idea Analyst and Associates, Inc.

"Lisa Pellegrene, President/CEO of Idea Analyst and Associates, Inc., developed the paradigm for a new kind of consultancy, where all business development and capital acquisition needs are met under one roof; simply put . . . one's ideas, concepts, and goals are refined and developed into one's reality. Ms. Pellegrene describes a new shift in our thinking . . . where we must allow ourselves to dream, and in that, simply realize that dreaming in and of itself is not enough. What is enough you ask? Have the courage to dream, to seek the knowledge, to perform the hard work necessary, and to place yourself in a position where good things may be bestowed upon you. Follow this path, and the dreams you desire may be small in comparison to what you are actually able to achieve. And lastly, . . . see what other people cannot, because you know what? At the end of the day, others will see what you believed. How do I know? Because I am happy to say I was a dreamer, still am . . . and I am learning that the word "dreamer" should and will, and in my opinion does, have a very positive connotation. This is the future . . . a world of dreamers. Imagine that. Just ask Ms. Taysha S.Valez."

Jennifer Wasson
Wasson Publishing Services

Wasson Publishing Services is a one-stop shop for all of your publishing needs—from copyediting and illustration to typesetting and book cover design. Jennifer's degree in design and illustration from the Kansas City Art Institute has provided her with the necessary skills to take on any book design and layout challenge. Her experience includes two years in layout, packaging, and logo design following by almost three years working for a small publisher where she helped in the production of books for the University of Phoenix, John Wiley & Sons, Inc., and McGraw-Hill Publishers.

To find out more about Jennifer's services and to see samples of her work, please check out her profile on ContractedWork.com at:

http://www.contractedwork.com/profile.cfm?portfolioid=366

You can contact her at 217.355.0445 or by email at:

jenniferwasson@hotmail.com

Thank U's

Thank you to Krystle Justine, my assistant and wonderful chef I might add. You make everything possible, chica. I love ya. You see order where others see chaos.

Thank you to everyone who helped me out:

My manicurist, Jennifer, from the Four Season salon; my best friend in the world, Kevin G.; Grandma; Mom; my girls and future millionairesses, Alana, Lisa. L., and Danielle Hamel; my printers; everyone at Kinkos; my wonderful editor, Jennifer Wasson; my great idea analyst; my accountants; and of course my bosses (a.k.a. the wonderful people who support my books, my nonprofit, my music, and in a nutshell, those who support my overall vision).

And to all the future supporters of Taysha S. Valez and the H.Couture empire, thank you in advance.

BYE!
Taysha Smith Valez

Basically, this whole book is an introduction—
an introduction to the wonderful world of entrepreneurship.

"Surviving when all odds are against you."

"This book is both inspirational and instructional."

"Did you know that a new millionairess is made
every sixty seconds? Are you next?"

I wanted to introduce myself as well as my series of business helpers in a UN lecturing way. If you read the author bio on the back of the book, you already know that I became a millionaire at the age of twenty-one because of my smart investments (i.e., real estate and diamond reselling) and ghostwriting ventures and that my purpose in life on this planet is to become a beauty and fashion mogul while helping others help themselves along the way. If only the journey was as sweet and to the point as the writing on the jacket of this book. The scary part is I am just beginning! There is nothing simple about business. Success in it is a product of tried and true hustle, hope, and planning. Entrepreneurship is one of the most empowering things a person could ever embark on. Owning your own and creating your own destiny. Signing your own checks! Whatever you want to call it. The process and learning to do it right is exhilarating, very complex, and long-winded all at the same time. If every detail about starting a business and developing it into a million-plus dollar success was published, the readings would be in volumes, each the size of the original *Moby Dick*. The *Young Black Millionairess*™ series was created for two reasons: 1) to shine light on an area that has so few role models for young women of color in business, and 2) to help every person help themselves one simple step at a time. The books are informative as well as entertaining. Nothing is watered down. Complex situations are made understandable because **a true Einstein knows** that the sign of a genius is one who can make the complex simple. Some say I make it look too easy and that I make it *sound* even easier, but I don't agree. I just want you to know that anything is possible and that nothing is impossible with the right tools. Thanks for buying this book, and I hope you become a part of the millionairess club. See you at the top!

Hello. My name is _____[your name here]_____ and I am a Millionairess/aire in training! (Keep this card at all times.)

Introduction

The following is from a speech that I wrote in college; I thought it would be helpful, almost like a kick-start to your millionairess education.

Ten things I wish I knew about me before I became who I am

I've always been the type of person who wanted to know but hated to be told—or so I thought. Until recently, I thought the questions that fueled my vehicle to dream were the cause of it coming to a dead stop. I would ask questions and hate the long-winded, overly-worded answers people were giving me, until one day it hit me like a sack of nickels—I hate to be lectured to. "Don't lecture me, just let me know." That became my motto. So when I asked any questions in the future, I would always end with the disclosure, "Don't lecture me, just let me know."

There were also other questions that I would ask myself that ultimately helped me reach my goals. That's when I realized that there are ten main things, ten things that are in all of us. If I had realized them sooner I would have been on the path to my destiny a lot sooner (with a map)!

1. I am creative (even though I am not a Van Gogh).
2. I have the power to change and shape lives.
3. I am a teacher.
4. I am forever a student.
5. I am worthy of all that is granted to me when I work for it.
6. If I do today what they said I could not do yesterday, tomorrow will they be doing it, too? (For sure!)
7. I am my biggest roadblock, critic, and dream crusher.
8. I am my biggest fan.
9. I am my own best friend.
10. I can do this! (Life, starting a million-dollar business, exercising, whatever!)

P.S. Oh yeah, by the way, starting a business and seeing it through to success is the hardest, scariest, most sleepless night thing I have ever done in my life. If that does not scare you, then continue reading and enjoy, but I warned you.

In my opinion, you should read this section first; it will be a great (business) language refresher.

Angel investor: A private individual who invests his or her own money in new enterprises.

Barriers of entry: Conditions that make it difficult or impossible for new competitors to enter the market; two barriers to entry are patents and high start-up costs.

Board of directors: The members of the governing body of an incorporated company. They have legal responsibility for the company.

Business plan: The blueprint of your business

Capital: The funds necessary to establish or operate a business.

Cash based accounting: An accounting method whereby income and expenses are entered on the books at the time of actual payment or receipt of funds.

Cash flow: The movement of money into and out of a company; actual income received and actual payments made out.

Collateral: Assets pledged in return for loans.

Conventional financing: Financing from established lenders, such as banks, rather than from investors; debt financing.

DBA: Doing business as a company's trade name rather than the name which it is legally incorporated; a company can be incorporated under 123 Corporation but do business as ABC Styles.

Debt financing: Raising funds for business by borrowing, often in the form of bank loans.

Distributor: Company or individual that arranges for the sale of products from manufacturer to retail outlets; the proverbial middleman.

Due diligence: The process undertaken by venture capitalists, investment bankers, or others to thoroughly investigate a company before financing; required by law before offering securities for sale.

E-business: A company that operates and exists primarily on the Internet.

E-commerce: Conducting sales and transactions through the Internet.

Equity: Shares of stock in a company; ownership interest in a company.

Exit plan: The strategy for leaving an investment and realizing the profits of such an investment.

Funding rounds: The number of times a company goes to the investment community to seek financing; each funding round is used to reach new stages of company development.

Going public: To issue an IPO (initial public offering).

Initial public offering: The first time the company's stock is sold to the general public (other than a limited offering) through the stock market or through over-the-counter sales.

Lead investor: The individual or investment firm taking primary responsibility for the financing of a company; usually brings other investors or venture capital firms into the deal and monitors the investment for all.

Licensing: The granting of permission by one company to another to use its products, trademarks, or name in a limited particular manner.

Limited partnership: An investment method whereby investors have limited liability and exercise no control over a company or enterprise; the general partners maintain control over a liability.

Market share: The percentage of the total available customer base captured by a company.

Milestone: A particular business achievement by which a company can be judged.

Millionairess: A woman who has a net worth of $1 million or more

Outsource: To have certain tasks, jobs, manufacturing, etc. produced by another company on a contract basis rather than having the work done by its own company in-house.

Partnership: A legal relationship between two or more individuals to run a company.

Profit margin: The amount of money earned after the cost of goods (gross profit margin) or all operating expenses (net profit margin) are deducted; usually expressed in percentage terms.

Sole proprietorship: A company owned and managed by one person.

Strategic partnership: An agreement with another company to undertake business endeavors together or on each other's behalf; can be financing sales, marketing, distribution, or other activities.

Venture capitalist: Individual or firm who invests money in new enterprises; typically this is money invested in the venture capital firm by others, particularly institutional investors.

Working capital: The cash available to the company for the ongoing operations of the business.

The dream team:

CEO: Chief executive officer (a.k.a. the visionary)

CFO: Chief financial officer (a.k.a. controller)

CIO: Chief information officer (a.k.a. Miss Technology)

COO: Chief operating officer (a.k.a. the team leader)

VPS: Vice president of sales (a.k.a. the star seller)

TRACK 1:
Are you that somebody?
(becoming an entrepreneur)

Are you ready to become an entrepreneur or millionairess?

This is a question that seems unnecessary, and I know you're probably thinking, "Why would I buy this book if I was not ready?" Most people have no idea how much hard work, dedication, and fine tuning goes into starting a successful business. Some people never get past the planning stage, or what I call the **"dreaming-and-I-can't-wait stage"**—"I can't wait until my business opens." "I can't wait until I am on TV or in magazines promoting my business." "I can't wait to move out of my ½ bedroom apartment into that house on the hills." "I can't wait until the world sees what I have to offer. It will knock their socks off." Eventually, "I can't wait" will become "I can't believe I actually"—"I can't believe I actually live in a house on the hills." "I can't believe I am in over forty magazines telling my story." But there is a LOT of work in-between. Are you up for the challenge? It will be hard, it might be easy, it will be fun and dreadful all at the same time. But if you plan right, manage right, and have what the people want, all I have to say is, "Meet you at the top!" One last question before we start: Are you that somebody?

What type of person does it take to own their own business?

I get this question a lot. It's not about the type because million-dollar business owners come in all different shapes, shades, and sizes. It's a matter of knowing yourself and knowing your weaknesses as well as your strengths. It's about embracing your weaknesses and understanding why they are indeed weaknesses and working at bringing them up to par with your strengths while maintaining your strengths. But if you must have an answer, me and all of the successful entrepreneurs that I've met all have these things in common: We are realistic, determined, creative, persistent, and we don't understand failure, only learning experiences.

Do I need a BA or MBA to run a successful business?

It wouldn't hurt. With those degrees you are more likely to become fluent in the language of business. You will know enough about "everything" regarding business. Education is freedom! However, is a formal degree absolutely necessary in order to build a successful business? Educators don't be mad, but I would say the answer is no. There are plenty of successful founders that don't have advanced degrees, *but* that does not mean you don't have to be educated. You will just learn the language on your own terms by seeking a mentor in your field of choice and/or reading every book and article and listening to every tape possible about your chosen field as well as general business. So in a since, you do earn your MBA, but from the university of you! In other words, there's no way around learning. The more you try to avoid it, the more problems you will come across, forcing you to learn the hard way. So whether you go to your local Ivy League, state university, or the university of you, do your best to learn to become fluent in your industry language as well as in the business language and you will be well on your way.

What if I fail?

Fail. What does that mean? Did you mean "What if my idea does not work out for me the first go around?" Did you mean "What if I have to stop midway because things are not developing as I planned?" "What if I have to reevaluate and start from scratch?" Well, if any or all of those things happen to you, I must say "Welcome to the world of entrepreneurship!" It's a crazy road. Nothing is guaranteed. Expect constant change, patience, and hard work. If it needs tweaking, tweak it. If you have to start over and plan again, start over. If you find yourself taking two steps forward and five steps backward with everything, reevaluate. Get help. Really listen and understand what went wrong and fix it. If this is too hard, ask yourself "Am I that somebody?" In other words, never ever, ever, ever give up!

How young is too young to start a business?

You are never too young to start your own business in my opinion. Age might seem like a burden or a catch 22 when it comes to years of experience in management, but do you want to know a secret? Most people don't know the true meaning of being a CEO. Yes, management is in the job description, but a CEO's main obligation is to have a vision and move the vision forward. She is responsible for building a team of people who have the experience and the know-how to bring that vision to life. She is the conductor, not the steel builder. I will talk about this more later on. Sometimes being young works in your favor. Father Time is not hanging on your back telling you that you will never have time to see your million-dollar vision turn into a million-dollar business. So embrace your youth and get to work. You have millions to make!

My support system is scarce. I don't have the luxury of having supportive family and friends. Should I still pursue my dream of owning my own business?

You better! Everyone's situation is different, but this is the true test of how bad you want it. Your situation will only make you stronger, and when you look back on all you've accomplished without the huge cheering crowd, you'll say "How in the world did I do it?" But do me a favor: Find one person—someone you can trust and someone who believes in you, whether it's a pen pal, a friend of a friend, or ME! Sometimes all it takes is one person to believe in you to help you make it to the next level. So don't worry. Just remember this little point about starting a business: "You will be too busy building your empire to worry about the small stuff." And believe me, it's all small stuff!

TRACK 2
Let's get it started
(The vision: What's your product or service?)

What type of business should I start?

That's tricky. Ask yourself these questions:

- What do I love?
- What do I live, eat, and breathe?
- What would I do business-wise even if I made no money from it and as long as my bills where paid?
- What am I interested in and what do I want to learn everything about in order to turn it into a business venture?

My best advice is doing it for the love—not the money, not the lure of riches and fame, not the lust. Do it for the love.

Ask yourself "What business do I really want to be in regardless of the dirty work?"

What are the different types of businesses?

There are many different types, but for now, I will mention two of the most popular.

- B to B (business to business): This is usually the type of business that sells a product or service to help out another business (i.e., consulting companies and wholesalers).
- B to C (business to consumer): This is the type of business that I am in and that most people plan to start. We sell our ideas, products, or services to the consumer who in turn, pays us for making their life easier, better, stronger, or a little brighter in some way, shape, or form.

What about buying a franchise?

Webster's Dictionary defines "franchise" as 1) A privilege or right granted to a person or a group by a government, state, or sovereign, and 2) Authorization granted by a manufacturer to a distributor or dealer to sell his products."

Franchising is a form of business in which the owner, or "franchiser", gives license to distribute products, services, or methods of business to affiliated dealers or "franchisees." In many cases, franchisees are given exclusive access to a particular geographical area. The franchiser usually mandates uniform symbols, trademarks, and standardized services.

Here is a history lesson. "Thirty years ago, franchising was a revolutionary new technology—a new and better way to retail goods, food products, and services to the consumers. How was it greeted? The media called it a scam. Headlines were everywhere about how some little old lady lost her life savings to some flim flam franchise. Major Fortune 500 companies were getting involved in franchising, but these companies insisted that their names not be used in ads or magazine stories.

Today franchising has turned into an $800 billion a year business. Experts estimate that today, as much as one-third of the goods and services in the U.S. are moved through franchising. It's hard to believe, but franchising actually came within eleven votes of being outlawed by Congress.

Essentially, a franchise provides a tested formula for starting a business that has worked for others. It can save you from making costly errors and can also shorten your learning curve.

Pros: Tried and true in most cases, and the failure rate of franchise owners is much lower than that of independent business startups.

Cons: Not all costs are given up front. Most people feel that they are cheated or unprepared when they see the final bill. A lot of people don't realize that the franchise fee is just that, a fee to franchise. In most cases, you still have to buy fixtures, lighting, land, and all other build-out materials. So don't assume that the low initial franchise fee is all that is needed in order to get your business off and running.

Note: I will get more into franchises in my book, *Young Black Millionairess™: To Franchise or Not to Franchise?* This book will cover every detail about franchise buying, selling, and creating. Franchising has a language of its own that cannot be taken lightly.

Now if you've already decided that this is for you, do your research. Start with your local library and check out these Web sites: www.franchise.com or www.financialadvice-usa.com. Plan and execute. See you at the top!

Most people decide to start a business based on such notions as "I love fashion so I am going to start a fashion line," or "I love music and parties so I am going to start my own record label," and "I love kids so I am going to start my own day care." That's all great, but it's not enough. Will they feel the same way when they see the high risk and small initial return that goes into starting a clothing line? Will they still want to open a day care when they realize all the licensing, zoning, and angry, unpleasant parents that come with it? And let's not forget about the kids who will always come back day after day. Will they still want to start a record label when they realize that it's 98 percent business and 2 percent art and music. If they answer "I don't mind," then it's love. If all you see is the back of their heads and smoke, then I guess they were in it for the lust and lure of luxury. From one millionairess to a future millionairess, do it for the love, not the lust.

Filling a niche

Nowadays, the only way to compete in any market is to find a niche, and sometimes you have to find the niche within a niche. Answer this question: What new things can you bring to the table that makes your business stand out? Sometimes the thing that sets you apart from the rest is, believe it or not, you! Once you figure out your niche, run with it and never look back!

You

What should I do as far as my own finances go to prepare for business ownership?

Great question. This is something that a lot of business owners tend to think about after it's too late. As soon as your vision is a twinkle in your eye, you should get yourself in order as far as your finances go. This includes paying your bills on time, building a strong relationship with your bank, and not abusing or over-extending your credit line. Start saving toward your dream. Start a savings account totally for your business. If you want to start a business five years from now, start saving five dollars a day toward that business. Don't touch that money. Put it in an interest-bearing account and watch your money grow. When you can put in more, put in more, but never go below your five-dollar-a-day rule. Do whatever you have to do legally to get that five dollars a day in that account. This is not just for saving, it's also a mental conditioning exercise. This will be training you forced discipline. And before you know it, you will have a good 10,000-plus dollars to work with. It might not seem like a lot, but it covers the minor things when you're getting started—everything from business cards to legal fees. And at the end of it you have a record, a clear, five-year record to show your bank. For those of you who want to start today, do the math. To start a business four years from now, start saving ten dollars a day. For a business three years from now, save fifteen dollars a day, and so on. You get the picture I am painting. The sooner you want to start, the harder you have to train. You have to pay for the time lost. My whole point is: get in the habit of making good habits.

Note: Check out the book *Young Black Millionairess*™: *Money: The Official Guide to Money—from Saving, to Credit, to Spending.* This book is a must-read for those who are trying to build a better financial future.

Is there anything I should do health wise in order to prepare for business ownership?

Yes. This is so important. Put that burger down and hit the pavement. Rent "8 Minute Body," "Butt Buster," and take a yoga class, whatever is within your budget and/or time to do because you will need to be in prime health in order to deal with the road ahead. It's like you're an athlete, and seeing your business through to that million-dollar success mark is like crossing the line at the New York City marathon in less than five hours! So ask yourself, "If I had to run the marathon tomorrow, would I be ready?"

What should I do appearance wise to get ready for business ownership?

Although some businesses are appearance dependent (i.e., the fashion and beauty world), no one is exempt from keeping up their appearance. Everyone knows that when you look good, you feel good, and when you feel good you are much more productive. Even if you're behind the scene and never in the public eye, you still have to dress the part, especially in the start-up phase. You will be the face and in most cases, the first impression to many who come in contact with your company, and you only have one chance to make a first impression.

*Sidenote: Ladies, you must get a "Power dress" custom fit by high-end designer, Tadine. I have seventeen of them, and they are a must for a millionairess or millionairess in training. Fellas, I did not forget about you. Tadine & Co. is known for their high-end custom tailored shirts and suits. Visit www.tadine.com.

What types of business education should I be pursuing to help me get ready?

Depending on your situation, the answer varies. Do you have the time and the resources to invest in a formal education? If not, workshops and your local bookstore are a great start.

What books, workshops, seminars, degrees, etc. should I be attending?

There are so many great seminars, degree programs, and workshops out there I could write a book on that alone!

Check out www.sba.gov and www.blackenterprise.com.

Fashion Institute of Technology has great inexpensive classes and a certificate on becoming a CEO and building your own business. However, if you're not close to New York, visit your local community college or university. More than likely, they will offer quick workshops and classes on how to start and grow a successful business. I will be conducting workshops and one-on-one training on DVD so you can learn and experience from the comfort of your own home.

Planning

Planning and building a team

I know you've heard it before: "You must plan—plans are your road maps to success." "Would you build a house without a blueprint or plan?" Yes, these lines are annoying, but true. The planning stage often weeds out the true from the wanna-be's. If you're not willing to take the time to plan, how are you going to find time to build a million-plus dollar empire? Just a question.

What is a business plan and why do I need one?

Producing the business plan is a critical stage in any new business venture Especially a million-plus dollar business venture! A comprehensive statement of the business objectives and how you intend to achieve them is essential, particularly if financing is required from outside the business.

There are no hard and fast rules about how to produce your plan—each one will be different depending on the nature of the proposed business.

A business plan:

- Organizes your thoughts and ambitions for your business venture.
- Uses a standardized format which can be easily read and understood by others.
- Tests the viability of your plans.
- Helps banks and others who might lend you money to see your vision.
- Provides a set of targets against which the progress and profitability of your business can be measured.

Although all plans should be tailor-fit for your company's needs, the following are general things that should be included in any business plans:

- A description of your business that defines exactly what you intend to do. Will your company plan red carpet launches of products? VIP water tasting sessions?
- The ownership and/or structure that defines the type of legal structure your business will operate under and why. S Corp.? LLC?
- The customers (a.k.a. your bosses). Who will they be? Will you concentrate on small corporations, large ones, or perhaps a particular market, say, up and coming women poets?
- The competition. Who offers a similar service? What are their strengths? A careful evaluation and list of competitors and their perceived strengths will help you to define your differential (a.k.a. your niche).
- The marketing strategy. How will you get the word out? What kind of advertising or promotion will you use? (Super important)
- Management. Who will manage the company and why are they qualified? (Super duper important)
- The financials. Often, a cash flow projection is all that's needed.
- An executive summary. This is language at the beginning that summarizes the plan. And, in most cases, is required as a separate document for investors to view before they review your full business plan.

Words of advice: Hire a consultant, accountant, and lawyer to write your plan. This is something that should be left to the pros. You can write a practice one on your own, but trust me on this one—a great plan is no solo project. It will make your life and your business a lot easier if you collaborate on this one! Just a suggestion. There are many tools and software packages out there to use as guides. With the time and dedication, I am sure the task can be done alone, but be ready to work, revise, and revise some more. Visit http://www.ideaanalyst.com and tell them Taysha V. sent you!

*Did you know the average business plan takes about 100 hours to write?

What is a strategic plan and why do I need one?

In strategic planning it is critical to formally consider how your organization will accomplish its goals. The answer to this question is a strategy. There are a variety of formal definitions for strategies, but everyone fundamentally agrees that a strategy is the answer to the question, "How?"

"Strategies are simply a set of actions that enable an organization to achieve results."

—MAP for Nonprofits, St. Paul, MN

"Strategy is a way of comparing your organization's strengths with the changing environment in order to get an idea of how best to complete or serve client needs."

—Jim Fisk and Robert Barron,
The Official MBA Handbook

Essentially, there are three different categories of strategies: organizational, programmatic, and functional. The difference among the categories is the focus of the strategy.

- Organizational strategy outlines the planned avenue for organizational development (e.g., collaborations, earned income, selection of businesses, mergers, etc.).
- Programmatic strategy addresses how to develop, manage, and deliver programs.
- Functional strategies articulate how to manage administration and support needs that impact the organization's efficiency and effectiveness (e.g., develop a financial system that provides accurate information using a cash accrual method).

What is a financial plan and why do I need one?

This is usually a part of the business plan. However, it is so important that I feel it should be able to stand alone as far as quality and detail go. It's basically the plan for your business's financial future. It helps you and your financial advisors (in most cases, your CFO and/or staff accountant) see where you're going and what needs to be tweaked. It's a map of your financial future.

What is forecasting?

Business forecasting offers a strategic method of planning for the future by predicting the direction in which your business is heading. Forecasting can involve simple formulas, such as the amount of clients you intend to have after a certain amount of time, or complex formulas that take into account a variety of different elements to produce a multifaceted prediction.

Today's business forecasting tools present a unified method of predicting for the future and offer valuable analyses by which to make the most educated assumptions. New software analyzes a plethora of different types of data and produces a comprehensive report regarding the overall financial health of your company and the industry as a whole. Understanding the importance of these predictions is the key to any successful business.

In the past, a team of analysts would often spend hours a day comparing notes and debating the meaning of volumes of seemingly unrelated data. It was indeed an inexact science, and often the sheer magnitude of the task produced results that were often fraught with error. A method of eliminating much of the human debate and ensuring an unbiased viewpoint became essential to a business's success.

Computer software accomplishes this goal by providing an entirely analytical viewpoint on the mountains of data and is able to unify thousands of interrelated formulas regarding the forecasting of business direction. These programs are able to take historical data and integrate it with current data to produce a collaborative and accurate enterprise-wide look at the overall success of the company.

What's with all the plans? Do I need them all in order to be successful?

No and yes. If you want to build and continue to grow a million-plus dollar business, plans are the way to go. The more organized in the beginning, and during, the more smoothly your business will flow. Would you want your contractor building your mansion and decorating it without a plan? I didn't think so.

What is a marketing plan and why do I need one?

The purpose of the marketing plan is to define your market, i.e., to identify your customers and competitors, to outline a strategy for attracting and keeping customers, and to identify and anticipate change. Your business will not succeed simply because you want it to succeed. It takes careful planning and a thorough understanding of the marketplace (let's not forget great instincts!) to develop a strategy that will ensure success.

*Having great instincts, paying attention to the world around you, and really listening to what the people are asking for is priceless.

Sometimes you need to plan to plan! All plans for your business are considered works in progress. Your initial plans will be tweaked and tweaked over the life of your business.*

Check out *Young Black Millionairess: Plans (Every Plan Your Business Needs in Order to Reach Million-Dollar-Plus Status)* Available winter 2005.

Who should write the plans? You, an accountant, or an MBA?

You, the accountant, *and* the MBA. It's a team effort.

The Team:

The number one reason for business failure is not lack of money-limited capital—that's number two. The number one reason is inexperience and/or poor management. You need to get this through your head right now. You are only one person. REPEAT AFTER ME: "In order to succeed I must look out and reach out to others for help." "I am not strong at everything." "I, as the owner, the creator, should also know my role." "If I don't have the experience or the know-how, I will find someone who does." "I will learn the language of my business and industry and all that it entails." "I will learn enough about everything so that I can delegate to and build a team of people who know everything in their specialized field." "I will find a team of people who live, breath, and eat their area of expertise. The latter is especially important in the case of trying to build a million-dollar business. These are the general people that you must have. I know you're saying that there are a lot of people who have made it without a team, but let me remind you, there are many more who have not. And always remember, you would rather be overprepared than underprepared.

Your team management:

- CEO: Chief Executive Officer. Usually the president, the founder, the visionary, the leader. A true CEO is more of a leader than a manager. He or she guides the team of managers to the next level. Their primary role is as leader and visionary.
- COO: Chief Operating Officer. This is the right-hand person. This is the person who runs the operating side, making sure everything is running smoothly and up to par.
- CFO: Chief Financial Officer. Also known as controller. This position is overlooked a lot of the time; however, it is wise to hire an experienced CFO who can help you maximize all your matters regarding your money. Sometimes the help of a CFO can be the final link to becoming a successful million-dollar venture.

Many business owners try to perform both the roles of CEO and CFO. However, both roles are extremely hard to perform simultaneously. When the head chief takes her eyes off of the horizon and starts to focus on the internal control issues, the business loses direction. However, without attention to systems and processes, the company will begin to wobble out of control.

- VPS: Vice President of Sales. Leads the sales team. Forms a strategic plan of action as to when, where, and how certain markets will be acquired.
- CIO: Chief Information Officer. In this day and age, this officer is a must. You have to be innovative in order to keep up with the time, and technology is the way to go.
- Director of Marketing. This executive is also a must. What are the differences between a known author and an unknown author? Publicity. A sold hat and an unsold hat? The marketing and the sales. The customer must know what you have to offer. More often than not, this is the missing link. A lot of people put tons of money into building but never any money into showing the house that they built. The director of marketing (along with the vice president of sales) helps create a successful strategic sales and marketing plan and sees to it that the plan is executed.
- Accountant. I would have an accountant for my personal finances and minor bookkeeping services. However, if your

accountant does not have CFO/controller experience, I would highly recommend hiring a CFO for major corporate financial and strategic planning.

- Lawyer. As soon as you say, "I have the best idea in the world for a business," start looking for a lawyer. Don't wait until you need a lawyer to start looking for one. Build a relationship with this person so that you know them and they know you. Very important.

- A doctor or physician on hand. Yes, you heard me right, a doctor. You will need to have someone you can trust just in case you get a pesky ailment. You can't let a cold get in the way of your success. That's silly.

Everybody's team is different. In the full-length version of the book I will explain the team that I have. Maybe your team will mirror mine or maybe it will be the complete opposite. The above team is a general one and a must if you want to build a million-dollar business. Some businesses need all of these positions filled; others don't (or so they think). I am talking from more of a business to customer type of business. A potential million-dollar empire will most definitely need all of these high-level positions filled in order to be successful, and most importantly, to remain successful.

Don't get caught in the trap of wearing every hat in the business. This will lead to burnout and basically more often then not, failure.

Note: Believe it or not, most, if not all of these team members can be hired on a part-time, as needed, or consulting basis. Do your research or contact your local interim executive agency.

My love doesn't cost a thing, but starting a small business will

Financing

I want to start this section with my experiences—how I financed my business, and my plans for financing it in the future. First off, I like to call the way I raised capital for my business the "Millionairess way." The Millionairess way is a combination of a few forms of financing depending on the stage of the business. If you haven't heard, most investors and banks like to lend money to those whose businesses are not money dependent. So I know you're asking, "How can I start a million-dollar business without capital?" My answer to you is, you will, in most cases, have to. Most investors do not invest in start-ups so you will have to get creative. Look for a way into your industry with the lowest possible entry while still maintaining quality. Grow and make a little money from that while all the while tweaking your business plan to show investors. People who lend money to others do so because they feel that the person or business will be a sure success. The more you hustle and believe in yourself and invest in yourself, the more others will want to invest in you and your business. Actually, your goal would be to fund all the stages of your business growth yourself without the help of outside funds. Oftentimes that's hard because of many factors (i.e., the right time to enter the market presents itself, but you're falling short of capital). You have to remember to open your brain and not put any limits on yourself.

Here is an example of what I did to raise capital. At sixteen-years-old I wanted to buy an $8,000 bangle. Of course my parents laughed at the thought of buying an $8,000 bracelet for a sixteen-year-old so I decided that if I wanted to get that bracelet, I had better get a job. I knew that working at the mall was not an option if I wanted to buy the bracelet before I turned sixty! So I hit www.craigslist.org. It had a different look and name I think, but it was what I had always heard people talking about when they were looking for new opportunities. So I logged on and started searching. I knew that I could not hold down a high-paying office job at sixteen regardless of how advanced I was so I started to look at all "virtual commute" jobs (i.e., all interaction takes place over the Internet). I realized through my search that most of the legit high-paying jobs were in the field of writing. I answered an ad that read "ghostwriter needed for a series of multi-racial children's books." I said to myself, "I know I can do this," so I responded to the ad. The woman who placed the ad was a well-to-do woman who was having trouble explaining in a good way to her young multi-racial children why they look the way that they do and what makes them so special. She loved my writing samples. She explained that the pay would be $40,000 in three installments, and that the book series would be anywhere from twenty to thirty short books. I almost died. $40,000 cash for a sixteen-year-old writing 80,000 words max. I took the challenge with confidence and succeeded.

That project lead to many other projects—nothing as large as the sum of the first, but all substantial lump sums. By age eighteen I was ready to invest my money into something else. One night while watching an infomercial about real estate, it clicked—"I can do this." So I went to craigslist.org again and typed the words "investment properties." I searched every major city. Atlanta had the most opportunities for first-time investors so that's where I started. I came across hardworking people who would rather give their house away than let the government take it away because of unpaid taxes.

My first investment came from a guy who owned his parent's house free and clear. All he had to do was pay the taxes. However, life got in the way and he found himself behind $9,000 in taxes. The township was at his door ready to put his house up for auction on a tax sale. I answered his ad, paid his back taxes, and he signed the house over to me for $1,000. The house had an APV of $289,000. I sold it six months later to his brother for $300,000. That was my first dealing with real estate. Since then, I have acquired many properties and sold many in the same manner. At one point, my real estate portfolio alone was $2.9 million.

With the money I made through real estate, I then went back to craigslist.org and typed in "diamonds." Guess what? A diamond reseller was looking for an investor/partner. He had the connections, all he needed was the cash. My first investment was that of $3,000 for an *x* amount of colored diamonds. With that investment we saw a return of $14,000, and split the profit. I have been working with this investor to build my portfolio ever since.

I then decided I needed to get even more creative and use what I have to take my business to the next level. I was always a pretty decent writer, so I decided to write all my know-how down. Once again, I hit the Internet and researched everything about publishing books. And here I am now—a publishing house owner and published author.

As we speak, I am tweaking my business plan so that I can present it to potential angel investors who are interested in my vision so that I can make this mogul dream of mine a reality. That was the short version of my story, but you get what I am saying. You have to have something to show before most will give a cent of their hard-earned money.

I have an amazing idea for a business but I don't have the money. What are my options?

You have so many options, but each one requires a different plan of action.

Equity financing (ownership)

Angel investors

University of New Hampshire Professor William Wetzel coined the term "angel investor," taken from the early 1900s practice whereby wealthy businessmen would invest in Broadway productions. Today, "angels" typically offer expertise, experience, and contacts, in addition to money.

Angel investors are individuals who invest in businesses looking for a higher return than found in traditional investments, and who often relish the thought of being a coach, a hands-on team member, or giving something back to the community. Many are successful entrepreneurs who want to help other entrepreneurs get their business off the ground. Angels usually provide the bridge capital from the self-funded stage of the business to the point the business qualifies for the level of funding provided by professional venture capitalists (VCs) or corporate strategic partners. An angel "round" of financing is typically $100,000–$1 million. Professional VCs average $10–$14 million per round, mostly in later stage companies, though a relative handful of seed stage VCs will fund smaller, earlier amounts, from $500,000 to $2.5 million.

With more than 2,500,000 individuals in the U.S. with a net worth in excess of $1 million, it is estimated that there are perhaps 400,000 active angel investors in the U.S. alone, funding 50,000 businesses per year. By comparison, professional venture capital funds about 5,000 companies each year. The total angel investment per year is estimated at about $40–$100 billion, about twice the total of all professional VCs. Also, there are at least 170 known angel groups throughout the United States. The Ewing Marion Kaufman Foundation in Kansas City has done research on business angel investing groups, along with William Wetzel at the University of New Hampshire's Center for Venture Research.

The "average" private investor is forty-seven years old with an annual income of $90,000, a net worth of $750,000, is college educated, has been self-employed, and invests $37,000 per venture.

Most angels invest close to home and rarely put in more than a few hundred thousand dollars.

Informal investment

Informal investment appears to be the largest source of external equity capital for small businesses. Nine out of ten investments are devoted to small, mostly start-up firms with fewer than twenty employees.

- Nine out of ten investors provide personal loans or loan guarantees to the firms they invest in. On average, this increases the available capital by 57 percent.
- Informal investors are older, have higher incomes, and are better educated than the average citizen, yet they are not often millionaires. They are a diverse group, displaying a wide range of personal characteristics and investment behavior.
- Seven out of ten investments are made within fifty miles of the investor's home or office.
- Investors expect an average 26 percent annual return at the time they invest, and they believe that about one-third of their investments are likely to result in a substantial capital loss.
- Investors accept an average of three deals for every ten considered. **The most common reasons given for rejecting a deal are insufficient growth potential, overpriced equity, lack of sufficient talent of the management, or lack of information about**

the entrepreneur or key personnel. There appears to be no shortage of informal capital funds. Investors included in the study would have invested almost 35 percent more than they did if acceptable opportunities had been available.

Venture capitalist (a.k.a. VCs)

Incubators are a type of venture capital company that invests in seed and early stage businesses and provides money along with connections and expertise in the field in which the new business operates. An incubator company's goal is to help you grow from concept to viable business enterprise. **Institutional venture capital** comes from professionally managed funds that have $25 million to $1 billion to invest in emerging growth companies.

> **Perfect for:** High-growth companies that are capable of reaching at least $25 million in sales in five years.
>
> **Best use:** Varied. From financing product development to expansion of a proven and profitable product or service.
>
> **Cost and funds typically available:** Expensive. Institutional venture capitalists demand significant equity in a business. The earlier the investment stage, the more equity is required to convince an institutional venture capitalist to invest. The range of funds typically available is $500,000 to $10 million.
>
> **Acquisition on a scale of 1–10 (1 being the easiest and 10 being the most difficult):** (9) Difficult. Institutional venture capitalists are choosy. The degree of difficulty is because of the fact that institutional venture capital is an appropriate source of funding for a very select number of companies.

Friends and family present a formidable source of capital. Your typical friend or family investor is male, has been successful in his own business, and wants to invest because he wishes someone had done it for him, according to Kirk Neiswander, director of entrepreneurial programs at Case Western Reserve University's Weather head School of Management. "They are not reckless investors, and they have shallow pockets," he says. "They will invest once but not a second or a third time and generally in an industry they know that is close to home. Typically, friends and family will invest up to $100,000."

However, investments with friends and family can turn out bad when things don't go as planned. The situation can be even worse than with professional investors because friends and family react to bad news as much with emotion as with logic. Take the following steps to protect everyone from each other:

1. Get an agreement in writing. This will eliminate all conversations that start with, "You never said that."

2. Emphasize debt (loans) rather than equity (ownership). You don't want friends and family in your company forever. Before you know it, they start telling you how to run the place, and long-buried emotions emerge. Make it a loan, and pay it back as fast as you can.

3. Put some cash flow on their investment. If Dad says, "Here's $50,000—try not to lose it, and pay it back as soon as you can," that's great. But consider paying some nominal interest at regular intervals so that you and he have a reality check. And it's better to pay this quarterly rather than monthly. This way, when things are teetering, your lender won't immediately know it.

Debt financing (loans)

Credit cards

They're not terribly creative. But credit cards are quick and easy. In a perverse way, they are also cheap. That is, a minimum payment of $50 per month can hold down a whole lot of debt. Of course, if you only make the minimum payment, your balance continues to grow, and if the business fails, you have to pay the piper. But if things go well and the business pays off the balances without missing a beat, then you look back at your early credit card financing with a nostalgic fondness, and perhaps a twinge of longing for simpler days.

Bank Loan

Bank term loans are the basic vanilla commercial loan. They typically carry fixed interest rates, monthly or quarterly repayment schedules, and a set maturity date. Bankers tend to classify term loans into two categories:

- Intermediate-term loans: Usually running less than three years, these loans are generally repaid in monthly installments (sometimes with balloon payments) from a business's cash flow. Repayment is often tied directly to the useful life of the asset being financed, according to the American Bankers Association (ABA).

- Long-term loans: These loans are commonly set for more than three years. Most are between three and ten years, and some run for as long as twenty years. Long-term loans are collateralized by a business's assets and typically require quarterly or monthly payments derived from profits or cash flow. These loans usually carry wording that limits the amount of additional financial commitments the business may take on (including other debts but also dividends or principals' salaries), and they sometimes require a profit set-aside earmarked to repay the loan, according to the ABA.

Perfect for: Established small businesses that can leverage sound financial statements and substantial down payments to minimize monthly payments and total loan costs. Repayment is typically linked in some way to the item financed. Term loans require collateral and a relatively rigorous approval process but can help reduce risk by minimizing costs. Before deciding to finance equipment, borrowers should be sure they can they make full use of ownership-related benefits, such as depreciation, and should compare the cost with that of leasing.

Best if used for: Construction; major capital improvements; large capital investments, such as machinery; working capital; purchases of existing businesses.

Cost and funds typically available: Inexpensive if the borrower can pass the financial litmus tests. Rates vary, making it worthwhile to shop, but generally run around 2.5 points over prime for loans of less than seven years and 2.75 points over prime for longer loans. Fees totaling up to 1 percent are common (though this varies greatly, too), with higher fees on construction loans. Typically, banks loan in amounts of $25,000 and greater.

Acquisition: (6) Challenging but sometimes a moderate challenge when smaller amounts are involved. However, for loans more than $100,000 (sometimes up to $200,000), you need a complete set of financial statements and must undergo a complete financial analysis by the lending institution.

Borrow against your home

This is the oldest trick in the book. It's also one of the best because you can exert almost total control over the process. Here's how it works: Say you need $50,000, your home is worth $250,000 and you owe the bank $100,000 on your mortgage. You can borrow against the equity, in this case $150,000.

Of course, once the loan kicks in, you'll have monthly payments. If you're starting a new business, it's a wise idea to set aside some of the proceeds from the home equity loan to help make these payments until the business can pay you a steady salary.

Another way to get money out of your home but maintain a lower monthly payment is to refinance the mortgage with a new one.

What are angel investors and how do I get one?

As I stated before, an angel investor is usually an individual that has funds to invest in a business. They are usually not as strenuous in the details and requirements as venture capitalists. They also usually invest in other industries besides pharmaceutical and technology. Keep in mind an angel can be anyone—your parent, your rich neighbor by default, any one person or persons who is looking to get "in" at the ground floor. Just because this type of founding source has the word "angel" in it, don't take it lightly. Angel means just that, angel. But they are still investors. You still have to come correct as far as business planning.

The process is not easy, but it is attainable. And because the angels can invest anywhere between $25,000–$2 million and more than one investor can invest in your company, the odds of securing your capital via this method is a lot more attainable. So if you need $2 million, split it up among various investors while paying close attention to the amount of equity in the company you are giving up.

Where do I find one or some? Angels and ventures can be found through groups and or personal recommendations. Like I said, a friend of your cousin's mom's sister could be looking to invest her

$5,000,000 in savings. Are you and your business that somebody to make her investments worth while? Investors also like projects that give them the option to grow. You know, just in case they want to invest in other "rounds" of your business past the start-up stage.

What are venture capitalists?

Venture capitalists are usually a group of high rollers who are looking to invest in moderate low-risk high-return business ventures, namely pharmaceuticals and technology. Sometimes it's hard to get the look or the handshake with a start-up that is looking for a million or less. But there are expectations to every rule.

Are there really grants and financing for minorities and women?

Yes and no. They are more like benefits. The myth of free money has left many disappointed. Most of the money goes to ventures that are not practical, but do your research. They might have a program just for you. Some programs have guidelines that seem impossible to meet, for example, you have to start a business within six miles of an Indian reservation and be first blood American Indian. I mean that might be you, but most likely it is not.

If so, where do I find out about these programs?

Do a Google search for grants for small business or visit www.sba.gov for information in your area. Beautywaterorg.com is a nonprofit that gives business grants at various stages of the business.

*BeautyWaterOrg.com provides grants to businesses with potential at all stages of the business. However, like any other source, you must have a solid plan of action. Visit www.beautywaterorg.com.

The SBA, how can that organization help me with financing my business?

The Small Business Administration

Term loans from a bank or commercial lending institution of up to ten years, with the Small Business Administration (SBA) guaranteeing as much as 80 percent of the loan principal.

Perfect for: Established small businesses capable of repaying a loan from cash flow but whose principals may be looking for a longer term to reduce payments or may have inadequate corporate or personal assets to collateralize the loan.

Best if used for: Purchasing equipment, financing the purchase of a business and in certain instances, working capital. The SBA guarantee can help borrowers overcome the problems of a weak loan application associated with inadequate collateral or limited operating history.

Cost and funds typically available: Comparatively inexpensive. Maximum allowed interest rates range from highs of prime plus 4.75 percentage points to prime plus 2.75 percentage points, though lenders can and often do charge less. These rates may be higher or lower than rates on no guaranteed loans. Even better, banks making SBA loans cannot charge fees (known as commitment fees) for agreeing to make a loan, or repayment fees, which means the effective rates for SBA loans may be, in some instances, superior to those for conventional loans. The SBA guarantees $50,000 to $750,000 of loan principal.

Acquisition: (8) Challenging. Although the SBA has created streamlined approaches to loan applications, conventional SBA guarantee procedures pose a significant documentation and administrative challenge for most borrowers.

How do you feel about using credit cards to finance a business?

They're okay, but should be more of a last resort. And I only say this because of the interest rates. But if that is the only way to get you off and running, then look for a low-interest business card with flexible terms.

Should I use my savings, 401k, etc. to fund my business?

Yes and no. Your savings and 401k are great to use because it shows other potential investors that you are wiling to take a risk in order to see your vision come to life.

What is bootstrapping?

Running your business with everything including the straps of your boot; operating on the minimal capital needed to start your company. The millionairess way is very similar to bootstrapping.

So you have the money

The fun has just begun!

Marketing, public relations, and branding

What should I include in my marketing plan?

Everything that has to do with getting your product and service to the people—what you have, why they will want it, and how you will get it to them.

What does branding mean exactly?

Most people think branding is a logo, a slogan, or even your company name. Those are all a part of it. But they're not all of it. Branding is planting your seeds in the minds of the people who are potential buyers of your product and service. It's about creating an experience. Creating that emotional connection that forces the consumer to connect your company with a specific aspect of their life.

What is public relations (a.k.a. PR) and how can it help my business?

Public relations is just that, your relationship with the public. It's communicating through print, TV, and radio. Public relations can be useful in every type of business. It creates the presence of referral rather than direct selling. It's very effective because of the soft sell approach. Hiring a public relations professional is a must for a million-dollar-plus venture.

What exactly is advertising?

Advertising refers to you, the seller, telling the consumer directly what you have to offer and why they should buy into it. Basically, advertising is less effective for start-ups. Because the prices for print, radio, and TV have skyrocketed over the years, there is no true benefit for the start-up company. I would recommend spending your money on a strong buzz marketing and PR campaign. Spending it on a one-time, $60,000 half-page glossy ad in *Vogue* is not wise for a start-up. This can be utilized later in the life of your company to maintain market visibility.

How do I develop brand identity?

A strong marketing plan and a strategic plan will help you form brand identity.

Is finding a graphic designer necessary?

Finding a graphic designer is cool. A graphic designer can make things easier as far as Web design, logo creation, etc. They often have connections to print houses and Web solution companies. It's more of a networking decision. If you are not a design guru, a graphic design service is relatively a dime a dozen and affordable.

How much should I spend on Web design and back-end services (services such as hosting, customer service, fulfillment)?

It depends. If your business is a Web business, plan as if you were building out a physical space. This is your business identity. If you're in the luxury goods business or entertainment business. plan to spend accordingly. Web design can run you anywhere between $1,500 and $50,000 depending on need.

Do I need a Web site?

Yes, it won't hurt. A Web site can be used to build your brand. A Web site can make your brand international without leaving your home state. Great as an information source as well as a commerce source. Some businesses make the bulk of their sales through their Web site and the power of the Internet.

Buzz marketing?

You heard it before—you have to create a buzz—the rumble before the storm. Buzz, in most cases, is more effective than advertising because most buzz marketing comes from word-of-mouth and people are more likely to buy if a product is suggested by someone they respect and/or admire. Most cult following products and services became such because of the power of buzz marketing.

Word-of-mouth marketing?

Is just that—marketing through the mouth. Example, your friend tries a product or service. She in turn, tells another friend who is the head of a booming online community. She tells that community and they tell their friends who tell *their* friends. IT can go on and on and is, in most cases, the most effective and inexpensive type of marketing.

Associative marketing?

Being involved with other product and service providers that are complementary to what you and your company have to offer. For example, if I am going to start a clothing line, I would want my products to be sold and advertised as allies with one or two other lines of the same genre.

Really knowing your market

This is so important. It requires research and true observation on your part. You really need to look and listen to what the people are asking for, not what you think they need. They have marketing research firms that can help with your analysis. However, research combined with instinct is almost foolproof and very powerful in serving your market I might add.

More than just age, gender, class, and ethnicity

Marketing to men versus women

Men and women are different and it should be that way. Stereotypes of pink, weak women and strong, blue men are changing. However, this is still a split market that has subdivisions within subdivisions of each.

- Research and utilize market research companies
- Do your own research: look, listen, and observe.
- Understand it's more about what they tell you they want than about what you think they want.

Know what business you're in so that your business will always be growing and expanding

Most people, when asked what business they are in, are not really sure of the question. They say things like, "I'm in the fashion business. I have my own clothing line," or "I am in the beauty business." When indeed you are in the business of helping people help themselves through fashion and/or beauty, the latter description leaves the door open for endless possibilities of growth within your "business," thus, leading to million-plus-dollar success.

This is very important when picking an industry or service or product. "Try to be first. Try to be the best. And build a brand that has international appeal. Or try to do all three."

Making it legal

Before you create any buzz or sell anything, you have to take care of the legal side of your business.

Note: The following is only general help information. It is not a substitute for legal advice. In otherwords, you must seek a lawyer for issues that require legal council.

Legal

What forms of business are there?

You have to form your business. And I know there are about a million business books on each. I will touch on all of them and really talk your ear off about the ones that would benefit a million-dollar business.

LLC: Limited Liability Company

Limited liability companies, or LLCs, are becoming more and more popular, and it's easy to see why. They combine the personal liability protection of a corporation with the tax benefits and simplicity of a partnership. In otherwords, the owners (or "members") of an LLC are not personally liable for its debts and liabilities, but also have the benefit of being taxed only once on their profits. Moreover, LLCs are more flexible and require less ongoing paperwork than an S Corporation.

As of October 1, 1997, Nevada joined with over forty states to recognize single member LLCs. Virtually all of the fifty States of the Union recognize multi-member LLCs. A growing number are giving the same recognition to single member companies. This gives the small business person all of the advantages of an LLC even though he or she is the only member. What are these advantages?

- It is a Tax Pass through entity like a partnership or Sub-S corporation.

- It offers its members all of the liability protection of a C Corporation.
- Its members are state tax free in Nevada.
- Under the "Check the Box" rules effective January 1, 1997, the taxpayer can elect to have his company taxed as a corporation or partnership.
- All fifty states recognize LLCs and forty of them recognize single member LLCs.
- This means that the tax advantages of Nevada will be recognized in your home state.
- You, of course, can have more than one member of an LLC. The structure of an LLC is different than a regular C Corp. in that there are member(s) and not shareholder(s). There is one main member called a manager, and that person has the same type of power as does the chairman of the board of a regular corporation.
- We suggest that if you are not sure of what type of entity to set up, set up an LLC. The reason for this is that you can change an LLC to a C Corp. without much trouble, but you will have some problems in switching from a C Corp. to an LLC.
- Also, in the first year or so, if the company has any losses, you can write them off your personal income tax return, and then when the company is making money, you can switch it to a C Corp., where the profits will be taxed at the low rate of 15 percent of the first $50,000 in profits. This way you can get the best of both worlds. This is a 100 percent legal move.
- At the end of each year, the LLC files a return with the IRS showing how much the profits or losses are and who the members are that get the credit for the losses or owe the taxes for the profits. The LLC does not pay taxes.

Source: From my notes from college and *The MBA Notebook* by Richard Price.

S Corporation

An S Corporation is the election of a special tax designation, which must be applied for and granted by the IRS to corporations that have already been formed. This election, in general allows for the income of the S Corporation to be taxed to the shareholder of the corporation as opposed to the corporation per se.

What are the advantages of an S Corporation?

The primary advantage of an S Corporation is the avoidance of double taxation. That is, the avoidance of payment of income tax on corporate net income, and then the payment of a further tax on the dividend income that is derived from the corporation.

An S Corporation allows certain income, deductions, and losses to be passed through the S Corporation to the individual tax return of each shareholder.

To elect S Corporation status with the federal government, the stockholder(s) complete form 2553 and mail or fax it to the IRS within seventy-five days of their date of incorporation.

This is the best solution for a home-based or small family business.

C Corporation

People tend to think of huge businesses like Ford or Firestone when they talk about C Corporations. But a C Corporation can also be the right vehicle for small entities.

The first and most obvious benefit of the C Corporation is that the corporation can deduct 100 percent of the health insurance it pays for its employees, including employees who are shareholders in the corporation. It also can fully deduct the costs of any medical reimbursement plan.

C Corporations also can deduct fringe benefits such as qualified education costs, group term life insurance up to $50,000 per employee, employer-provided vehicles, and public transportation passes.

A second potential advantage of C Corporations is the tax rate applied to modest profits. The first $50,000 in annual profits is taxed at a rate of 15 percent. By comparison, anyone with taxable income that high is seeing at least part of it taxed at 28 percent.

If the corporation has profits after paying all of its expenses (including your salary), the corporation pays tax on those profits. When the profits are distributed to you as a shareholder, you pay personal income tax on the dividends. This combination of a corporate income tax, followed by a personal income tax, is commonly referred to as double taxation.

Many small businesses have little left in the way of earnings after salary and the fringe benefits are paid out. Little or no earnings mean little or no corporate taxes or double-taxation issue.

Losses get held in a C Corporation and aren't passed through annually to shareholders, which can make other forms, like S Corporations more attractive to people who want to claim losses on their personal returns. In addition, tax rates and considerations change rapidly as C Corporations get more profitable. The marginal rate escalates to 39 percent at the $100,000 income level.

Sole proprietorship

A sole proprietorship is a business that is owned by one person and that isn't registered with the state as a corporation or a limited liability company. Sole proprietorships are so easy to set up and maintain that you may already own one without knowing it. For instance, if you are a freelance photographer or writer, a craftsperson who takes jobs on a contract basis, a salesperson who receives only commissions, or an independent contractor who isn't on an employer's regular payroll, you are automatically a sole proprietor.

However, even though a sole proprietorship is the simplest of business structures, you shouldn't fall asleep at the wheel. You may have to comply with local registration, business license, or permit laws to make your business legitimate. And you should look sharp when it comes to tending your business, because you are personally responsible for paying both income taxes and business debts.

Personal liability for business debts

A sole proprietor can be held personally liable for any business-related obligation. This means that if your business doesn't pay a supplier, defaults on a debt, or loses a lawsuit, the creditor can legally come after your house or other possessions.

What about copyrights, trademarks, signature marks, patents, etc.?

Intellectual property, often known as IP, allows people to own their creativity and innovation in the same way that they can own physical property. The owner of IP can control and be rewarded for its use, and this encourages further innovation and creativity to the benefit of us all.

It will often not be possible to protect IP and gain IP rights (or IPRs) unless they have been applied for and granted, but some IP protection such as copyright arises automatically, without any registration, as soon as there is a record in some form of what has been created.

- Patents for inventions—Needed for new and improved products and processes that are capable of industrial application
- Trademarks for brand identity—Needed for goods and services allowing distinctions to be made between different traders. Your trade name is the name your company will be known as, not necessarily your legal formation name. For example, Love Body LLC could have a trade name "Singles Station."
- Designs for product appearance—of the whole or a part of a product resulting from the features of, in particular, the lines, contours, colors, shape, texture, or materials of the product itself or its ornamentation
- Copyright for material—Needed for literary and artistic material, music, films, sound recordings, broadcasts, and software and multimedia

However, IP is much broader than this, extending to trade secrets, plant varieties, geographical indications, performers' rights, and so on. To understand exactly what can be protected by IP, you will need to check the four main areas of copyright, designs, patents, and trademarks as well as other IP. Often, more than one type of IP may apply to the same creation. In otherwords, you and your lawyer need to have a talk.

When should I consult a lawyer?

As soon as you decide you want to be in business. Try to find a business lawyer who has experience with intellectual property.

$\mathcal{M}$oney accounts issues—
Be your own CFO or find a good one

When should I hire an accountant?

An accountant is great for basics such as bookkeeping and taxes. A great accountant can save you time and money in the long and short run in both your business and personal life. An accountant can also help with the legal structuring of your business. I would hire a CPA based on a recommendation. This is your money we're talking about. We can't have any ol' Jake or Jane handling your money. Seek out other business owners who have a good report and ask what account-ant they use and trust.

What about QuickBooks?

QuickBooks is cool for the do-it-yourselfer, but for the millionairess I would use it for personal uses. It's not capable of handling the requirements of a multi-million-dollar venture. Great tool, though.

What is a CFO and do I need one?

The role of CFO can differ from company to company depending on the type and size of the business. However, one constant is that the CFO is an integral part of the senior management team. The func-tional duties of a CFO are as follows:

- Financial statements
- Cost accounting, credit and collection
- Internal control
- Supervising the accounting staff
- IT or HR responsibilities
- Banking
- Special analysis and reports

A chief financial officer (CFO) is often overlooked. Why? I don't know. Because of the current job climate, a CFO is easily accessible;

CFOs are available virtually, part-time, or on an as-needed basis. If your million-dollar start-up can't have a CFO onboard as a salaried employee, at least they could have them on for an hour. Plan for it. The expertise of a CFO could be the difference in your company becoming a negative or positive statistic. Never make anything bigger than you. Every tool you need is available and reachable. You just have to make it happen for you.

Are bookkeeping services necessary?

Yes and no. I would say your accountant could handle any bookkeeping you needed. A separate service might be a waste of time.

Beating the stereotypes of African Americans and Latinos: Can you believe they said that?

African Americans and Latinos are known to make it big for one of two things in the media: entertainment and sports. It's often glamorized and criticized all at the same time. It's like our way out. Our way out from the poverty, from the slums, so they say. "So what, we happen to like music." "So what, we love sports." But do they ever talk about the 40 percent of African Americans and Latinos who are in college at the top of their game learning the language of these fields? Do they ever talk about them being doctors, lawyers, teachers, and CEOs, all at the highest level of their game? No. Why? Because it's not entertaining. The only things they ever talk about are extremes because extremes are entertaining. Extremes sell newspapers. Extremes get ratings. For example, would anybody really be reading this book if I were not a young, black (of Dominican and Native American descent) millionaire? Would they really be interested in anything that I have to say about business although it's sound, simple advice. Maybe, but I doubt it. I am an extreme young, black (Latino and Native American) millionaire at the age of twenty-three! A beauty and fashion mogul in the making. Someone who is ready and willing to tell all her secrets, all her struggles to make it work. In my opinion, we need these entertainers and sports people to keep on playing. We need all the positive determined goal-driven people as role models almost as a sense of hope. And I do sense forward movement toward diversity of these role models. Soon it will be cool to be a publisher and a writer when it's glamorized as an extreme to freedom. Because that is what we want—freedom. Money gives freedom. Education is freedom. Knowing is freedom. No longer are the days of the lonely musician who dies not knowing how to conduct business in the multi-billion dollar industry. We, the extreme, have taken a huge part of the pie. We are the ones who are really making the money through leverage and education and understanding. We no longer just play; we are making the rules and playing the game like it's never been played before. To all the media, thank you and shame on you at the same time. You make us stronger, wiser, and more successful. Everyday you show us the youth that without you we would be nothing .We don't control you (yet) and we do respect your hustle. And realize you are our allies, whether forced or voluntary. So ballers, ball. Entertainers, dance and sing us all the way to the top, but just don't forget that all eyes are on you (and me) whether you like it or not, so make the correct choice with your actions.

That's my piece.

Kisses, Taysha V.

TRACK 9:
E-commerce

Young Black Millionairess™:E-business—Using it to leverage your brick and muter or as an entity in its own. Will be a full-feature book fall 2005.

For E-business you must have an affiliate network and benefits; you must be affiliated with a good source.

Starting and operating an Internet business is surprisingly similar to operating any other business. Good business practices, like building the confidence of customers through truthful advertising, providing products and services at a fair price, and developing long-term business relationships, are as applicable to Internet businesses as they are to any other businesses.

Having said that, there are some important differences related to Internet businesses.

- Low start-up costs—When you decide to start a business online, you can do so with as little as a few hundred dollars and a good idea. However, don't be misled into believing that the Internet is an arena for instant riches with little or no effort. Nothing could be further from the truth. Like any business, it takes creativity, planning, money, and hard work to be successful.

- Multiple skill requirements—Suddenly it's not enough to simply have a good product or service. To use the Internet effectively, you now need to have or be able to acquire skills in graphic design, web server technology, programming, and a brand new marketing medium, not to mention skills needed in multi-lingual translations, international accounting and legal issues. Fortunately, it is not necessary that you have all this knowledge yourself. With the right combination of strategic partners and associates, all of these skills are easily found, if you know where to look.

- Endless marketing possibilities—The opportunities and ease of fostering strategic alliances to bolster marketing efforts is unsurpassed on the Internet. The reason we see so many cooperative relationships between companies online is that doing so has become so simple and so profitable. The advertising industry has found itself with many more possibilities as well as significantly more competition.

- Easily traceable results—Another byproduct of business on the Internet is that tracking potential customers as a group and visitor preferences is an ordinary part of business on the Internet.

- International audience—Even if you do not think of your business as an "international business," you must recognize that your visitors are likely to be from all over the world. You should consider whether or not you are prepared for international shipping and other transactions with countries other than your own. You should also strongly consider having your Web site translated into languages other than English. The percentage of non-US businesses on the Internet has risen dramatically in just the past year!

- Professional look—A professional-looking site is a must in this day. More often than not, your Web site is your storefront and/or the only connection some of your customers have to your business. A professional-looking site gives your potential customers a sense of security.

Source: Starting an Internet Business by Krystle Mason. Copyright cleared.

You don't need a lot of money to be successful in Internet business, although it is not realistic to expect to do it for free. Even small, home-based Internet businesses that can fill a niche can operate successfully and profitably. The number one mistake someone thinking of starting an online business can make is to think too broadly, and/or to try immediately to sell products to other people that teach them how to start an Internet business. Ironically, many people with no knowledge whatsoever seem to think that they can teach others how to do what they, themselves, have not accomplished.

The Internet, e-marketing, and e-commerce *can* make a lot of money for you. You need to have a niche to fill, then design, buy, or represent as an affiliate a product or products to fill that niche.

That said, how does one go about starting a business online? There are four general types of Internet businesses that you can start.

- A portal site or a portal that sells digital products
- An e-commerce business that sells a digital product
- An e-commerce business that ships tangibles to people
- A business-to-business and/or service-selling Web site

In addition to the above, you can also start either an affiliate marketing business, or can do network marketing online. In both cases, you can start and run these types of online businesses with or without a Web site.

One other type of Internet business or Web site is called "brochure ware." This is a site that acts as an online catalog for your company or organization, but from which people can't purchase online. These sites do serve a purpose but have very little to do with running an online business for profit, so we won't be discussing them.

Okay, let's dive in and see some examples of successful online businesses.

Portal sites or portals, which sell digital products

This is a very exciting model that requires mostly knowledge and time. A portal site is a site that provides information to people for free, or for a fixed price, and sells digital products to site visitors. You might be asking yourself, "How do I create a portal?" or "Do I have what it takes to build a portal site?" To build a successful portal you need the following:

- A lot of information to share on a particular subject that people are interested in. If you have this, then creating a portal site can just be plain fun and sometimes very profitable.
- You need to learn how to build and edit your own Web site.
- A product of your own creation, or products you advertise as an affiliate, so that you can "monetize" (i.e., earn income from) your Web site.

One man, in particular, specializes in teaching people how to create and run successful portal sites (he calls them "content sites", but they are really the same thing). If this type of site interests you, you owe it to yourself to learn about Internet business at www.sitesell.com. This is some of the most solid information you can find on how to run an Internet business, and the cost is a fraction of what many other people charge for information that is of lesser quality and lesser volume. You simply cannot go wrong following Ken Evoy.

The truth is, you don't need a lot of money to build and launch a Web site! You can start your first Internet business with an investment as small as a few hundred dollars. Where else in the world can you open a business with worldwide exposure for so little? Only on the Internet! The Newbie Club (www.newbieclub.com) is an example of a great portal site dedicated to helping people who are new to running a business on the Internet. Their Web site is not only a portal, but they also sell their own digital products to club members and nonmembers. This type of Web site, a portal that sells digital products, is really the wave of the future. Most of the products available at the Newbie Club are related to how to use computers and how to use the Internet effectively.

Examine the site layout and content. Their design is very deliberate and straightforward. Visit this Internet business information site and see for yourself. This is a classic, high-quality portal site.

By looking over this site, you'll not only learn about how to start an Internet business, you may even find a product or two that will help you. This is a very popular site for people who are interested in Internet business start-ups, for good reason. The content and products are first rate!

The site www.ybmillionairess.com is also a portal site that sells digital products on entrepreneurship. The information is free to members. Paid membership is required in order to receive free information and substantial savings off of digital products and services. Many of the links on the site suggest and recommend products through affiliate links, which means the site earns a small commission when you purchase the suggested products through the link.

E-commerce business site that sells a digital product

This is becoming a very common approach to selling on the Internet. Imagine having a downloadable digital product, like an e-book or software program, that can be sold online. All you have to do is find the market that needs this product, create the product at the highest quality, set up your Web site, and start raking in the money. Yeah, right!

This isn't all that difficult, but neither is it as simple as some people make it sound.

This type of Web site consists primarily of what is known as a "sales letter," and is often referred to as a mini-site, since it contains only a few pages, primarily the sales copy, and the ordering page. The sole purpose of this site is to move you to purchase the product. You will notice that the design is very different from the design of the typical portal or "content" site. The entire Web site is automated, including the pages for purchasing and downloading the e-book and entering the private area of the site.

An example of a more ambitious sales site is an online bookstore, which features e-marketing e-books and software such as www.hcoutureibooks.com.

An e-commerce business that ships tangibles to people

This is probably the most common platform that people use to start an online business, and also one of the most difficult. Trust me, I know. This type of Internet business is more familiar to most people than the portal and content sites discussed earlier. Most people find the concept easier to relate to because they are accustomed to buying and selling tangible products in the offline world, and most people have bought something over the Internet. There are thousands of large businesses using this standard e-commerce model. A great example of a small business using this model is the Web site of Maritza de la Guardia, www.beautygram.com. This site is run by a self-proclaimed handbag and beauty product junkie.

An increasingly popular variation on this model is to sell drop-shipped products, either through a direct-sales Web site, or by using online auctions, such as e-Bay. For many people, this is a simple and lucrative e-commerce model.

A business to business Web site

In a nutshell, a "B2B" Web site offers a product or service that other online business owners need and use. It could be an ezine directory, traffic generation, accounting services, autoresponders, or countless other things. In a sense, this is a very shrewd business move, since your target market is not the general public, but other business owners. You know they have money to spend, and you know they need your product, and you know where to find them. By doing Internet business "B2B," you've solved many of the dilemmas faced by people trying to start an Internet business, or any type of business for that matter.

Another service that many Internet business owners need, especially if they intend to do any aggressive e-marketing using e-mail, is an autoresponder. The Internet continues to spawn more and more services geared to helping other Internet business owners succeed. If you want your Web site to be seen by Web surfers, you need to understand what key words or phrases people are using on the search engines to find your type of product or service. Wordtracker (www.wordtracker.com) has created an affordable service that allows you to research the optimum phrases and words to use for your Web page title and your key phrases. This is another great example of an Internet business selling services.

I don't have a product, but I want to start an Internet business!

If you, like most people, have the desire, but no idea where to start, you have a couple of choices. One is to take up either affiliate marketing or online network marketing, and represent someone else's product for a commission. Most people doing this don't make a great deal of money, but those who are dedicated have a shot at the elite, that 5 percent or so of whom become "super affiliates" or "network superstars" and do extremely well.

Affiliate marketing can also provide a great second income stream, if you already have a Web site and can pick up some products to represent as an affiliate. Your goal, of course, is to find products that complement rather than compete with or contradict the theme of your existing Web site.

Regardless of whether you're an Internet business "newbie" or a Web site owner looking for additional income, you can find tons of products to represent at two of the biggest affiliate marketing portals, www.clickbank.com and www.commissionjunction.com.

A more lucrative way to start an Internet business is to develop and sell your own info-products. In the long run, this is a better approach to starting an online business because you own and control the product, and instead of competing with hundreds or even thousands of other affiliates, you are only competing against those with similar products.

If you're going to create your own products, though, you really need to do some research and find an Internet business niche. It's been said that "the riches are in the niches," and it's absolutely true.

Well, we've covered a lot of territory already. Now it's time to start thinking about Web site design.

I'm a firm believer in the old adage that "knowledge is power," and I personally think that a few dollars spent on a couple of good references will pay off in the long run.

For more on this topic, check out *Young Black Millionairess*™: *E-Business: How to Start and Run a Million-Dollar Business or Two!*

This section is special. It consists of small thank-you notes to women of color whom I respect as well as admire the most. These women have unknowingly helped me reach my current status while also helping me to reach far beyond my preconceived capabilities.

- Kimora Lee Simmons: Founder of the Baby Phat fashion empire. (Fashion icon)
- Jonnetta Patton: CEO/President of J-Pat Management. The brain behind Usher Raymond's success (music icon)
- Oprah Winfrey: If God was a woman on earth in entertainment, her name would be Oprah. (philanthropist)
- Jennifer Lopez: Miss J.Lo; Founder of Sweet Face Inc. She shows that a woman can be great in both the arts and business (art and commerce icon)
- GMA: My beautiful grandmother, who is a product of what hard work can produce no matter what the odds. This woman would give her left foot to help me succeed, and I love her for that. (the survivor)
- Mami: The person who birthed me. My teacher and my counselor (the teacher)

Dear Kimora,
You are a true inspiration. You embody hip hop glam. But beyond the flawless diamonds and the perfect silhouette lies a true beauty. You make it look easy, girl. You've opened up doors for women of color, especially bi-racial women of color, that might have never been opened. You taught me that I don't have to choose. That I can embrace and incorporate all of me into my business and creativity. I want to say thank you for being you. Thank you for showing that with hard work anything can be done and done with style.
Love ya,

Taysha Valez

Dear Miss Oprah, (Can I call you "O"?)
All I can say is, you're amazing. Thank you so much for being you. Thank you for showing the world that beauty starts from the inside out. You are a model in all that you give, share, and teach. I am forever your student. Can't wait to talk to you on your couch someday. I have some questions to ask you. Wow, a billionairess! That is amazing Miss O. You've shown me that the sky is truly not the limit. It's just the beginning. Thank you.
Love ya,
Taysha Valez

Dear Ms. J-Pat,
What can I say? You have really paved the way for women executives in the music business. People have no idea how much of a "baller" you are. You are doing your thing and I love you for that. Always humble and always in style, never trying to steal the spotlight which you so deserve. By the way, you did a fine job with Mr. Raymond IV. You've shown me that no matter how much the odds are against me or how much of a "minority" I am in any industry, I can still wind up amongst the best, and in most cases, leading the pack. I hope to work with you in the near future, if you'll have me of course. Thank you so much for being you.
Love ya,
Taysha Valez

Dear Ms. Lopez, (or J. Lo for short)
You are in inspiration to Latinas everywhere. I love you for that alone. For one, I admire you for your drive and determination. You've shown me that I can be a success in both the arts and business. Thank you so much mama. Thank you again for being you.
Taysha Valez

Hey G-Ma, (Grannie)
Just wanted to say thank you. Thanks for believing in me when nobody else did. Thanks for listening to me ramble on about all my crazy ideas. Thanks for helping and funding all of my creations. Just thank you so much for showing me what a strong woman really is. I thank you and I love you for that.
Bye
Love you much
Tazy

Hello Mami,
You are the most important of all the ladies. You are my mentor, my inspiration, at times when you think I know it all naturally. I just make it look that way. I learned it all from you. I appreciate everything that you have done for everyone and are still doing for me. You knew I would make it before I did. Don't want to get cheesy, but thanks, and I love you.
Tazy

Taysha S. Valez bio

Taysha, at twenty-three, is the CEO of H.Couture Beauty LLC and the nonprofit H.Couture Beauty Water Inc. (a.k.a. www.beautywaterorg. com). Through untraditional education (Taysha calls herself a self-proclaimed workshop and certificate junkie) she has honed her skills in the areas of beauty, fashion, and business. Taysha became a millionairess through her investments (i.e., real estate and diamond reselling) and ghostwriting ventures while in college. "I did it all over the Internet. The Internet leveled the playing ground. I was so sharp and polished that people just believed in me and doors started to open. I've never looked back since!" Before deciding to become a fashion and beauty mogul, Taysha was on the path of medicine. She spent a brief stint as a behavioral therapist before starting her company in the spring of 2004. Currently pursuing her education in various fields, Taysha is also a young executive member of the prestigious CEW organization in New York. Taysha's philosophy in life is "Love what you do, share what you know, and always dream your dream." Taysha is a young mogul in training, persistent and focused. Her expertise in the beauty and business worlds is precise; she is armed and ready to take over the beauty and fashion world one body part at a time. Although labeled the Princess of Eyebrows in her teens, she does not want to be boxed in to a title. She wants to carve a spot in history for herself by being a teacher, author, artist, philanthropist, and entrepreneur—a full mogul in the true sense of the word, an inspiration. Taysha has a passion for beauty, fashion, business, and people, and because of her diverse cultural background, she is not one-dimensional. She is currently in discussion with investors, the best chemists, manufacturers, and distributors in the business. Taysha has this to say: "Look out for H.Couture. We plan to be here for a long time and on the lips, literally, of the people. We plan to change the model of business, fashion, beauty, and professional workings as we know it." Taysha still plans to pursue her goal of becoming a psychologist. "If I have the time, maybe when I am forty-five, I will tap back into the medical world so that I can help those who need a little help helping or finding themselves." Taysha also has plans to pursue her certification to become a diamond grader through www.gia.edu and is currently attending Berklee College of Music to complete her master certification in songwriting.

ℋ little about H.Couture Beauty LLC

H.Couture Beauty LLC is not just a beauty company; it's a lifestyle brand and empire in the making. It includes and represents everything from how-to-do-it-right books on beauty and fashion, to a designer water that, of course, is called Beauty Water. H.Couture Beauty LLC was officially formed in February 2004. However, the company has been in the making since 1994. After years of continuous research and development, the first products of this innovative company are ready to be unveiled. CEO and founder, Taysha Valez, formed the company. Only twenty-three years old, Miss Valez, who prefers to just be called Taysha, is finally open to share her vision of the fusion of the fashion, beauty, arts, and professional world. The "H" in H.Couture stands for "Hiphotica"—meaning, "Hip Hot" and the "ica" adds a tré femme touch to it. Couture, of course, is there because it's the best, and all her products and services seem as if they were custom-designed for each individual customer. The musical note that topped the signature diamond Swarovski crystal symbolizes Taysha's passion for the arts and her love of music as well as diamonds! It also is a symbol of homage to some of her main influences: Miss Kimora Lee Simmons, the creator of the urban femme brand Baby Phat Inc.; Russell Simmons, the godfather of hip hop and urban entrepreneurship; and many others—among them the late but forever great, Estée Lauder, who indirectly taught Taysha never to be afraid to offer too much in this business we call beauty and fashion as long as it's needed for quality. With that in mind, Taysha has created a true lifestyle company that includes a beverage company, publishing firm, full cosmetics line, a luxury nail care line, fashion house, prestige fragrance line, and a sure-to-be-trendsetting plan to develop a franchise of brow boutiques and pedicure salons around the country, and eventually, around the world in order to provide other women and minorities the opportunity to become entrepreneurs themselves. To an apparel line that embodies everything, H.Couture stands for the comfy, fashionable, easy-to-wear, and necessary. Because of her age, she not only nurtures the trends the consumers follow; she is also a model and a consumer herself. Taysha is no novice in the world of beauty; her education is quite impressive. Taysha is also at all the big-name trade shows such as Health & Beauty America (HBA) in New York and Cosmoprof in Europe. She is also a young executive in the prestigious Cosmetic Executive Women (CEW) organization. Taysha also has a background as a behavioral therapist. This profession has taught her how to understand people as a whole, and why they react the way they do.

H.Couture has so many dimensions; it's almost overwhelming. Following are brief descriptions of a few divisions of the H.Couture Empire.

H.Couture Beauty Water Inc. (the nonprofit organization that I own) www.beautywaterorg.com

Who would have thought that water would become the new cosmetics breakthrough? The new beauty must-have? It's the magic beauty potion—the key to weight loss, beautiful skin, and longevity in life.

H.Couture Beauty Water™ is a prestige designer artesian water. It has undergone a triple ultraviolet light filter and is packaged with the same matriculation as a prestigious wine. This beauty water product prides itself on its purification and taste assurance process. The water, as mentioned, is triple UV-filtered in order to kill any bacterial contamination. To ensure longer shelf life and premium taste, the water is ozone-treated, a process that ensures freshness, eliminates the use of chemicals such as chlorine, and is sodium-free. What really sets this water apart from the rest is the packaging. It is styled the true "H.Couture way" in a premium glass silhouette-styled bottle with a platinum-topped, dressed diamond Swarovski crystal. H.Couture figures that if you are going to carry it anytime anywhere, it might as well complement your outfit. With all the boyish sports-inspired bottled waters out there, H.Couture Beauty Water™ is surely to live up to its reputation as the best-dressed water in the biz. Drink up. H.Couture

Beauty Water is the official water of BeautyWaterorg.com nonprofit organization

Beautywaterorg.com is located in Beverly Hills, California, as well as in New York City, New York. The goal is to raise funds for AIDS awareness, breast cancer awareness, literacy, business ownership grants and education grants, and scholarships using designer artesian bottled H.Couture Beauty Water as the tool. H.Couture Beauty Water will serve not only as a bridge to unite people to support the aforementioned causes, but will help people recognize that being a beautiful person is about helping people help themselves—that it is everyone's responsibility to help others who are in need through teaching and overall support.

Coming soon in summer 2005 at www.beautywaterorg.com and specialty beauty retailers, luxury hotels, spas, and fine beverage establishments.

Talk about being busy. Taysha is truly ahead of her time, a definite beauty and fashion mogul in the making.

H.Couture Publishing

The publishing house of the future. H.Couture Publishing is a mix of classic publishing with a twist of modern publishing. H.Couture prides itself on its ability to find diamonds in the rough and shape them into superstars in the literary world. The genres that H.Couture deals with are self-help, beauty, fitness, humor, and cookbooks.

Niche publishing at its best, H.Couture Publishing is the safe haven for information, self-help, and humor. H.Couture Publishing stands apart from the crowd by embracing developing promising new writers, something that is unheard of in this day and age. The first line-up from this innovative publishing house includes: The YBMillionairess (Young Black Millionairess™) Business Series, a string of humor books by various authors to lift the spirit, and a few self-helps on the subjects of engagement to eyebrows.

0511 Publishing

H.Couture Publishing recently acquired 0511 Publishing, formally owned by Kevin Gordon (who will remain CEO of 0511 Publishing) to create a more masculine presence to the H.Couture Publishing family. The 0511 Publishing division will release Young Black and Schizophrenic, a collection of works from black and Hispanic youths suffering from mental disorders, and on a lighter note, How to be a G: A Guide to Becoming a Modern Day Gentleman.

www.0511publishing.com
Genres: poetry, self-help, cookbooks, mental health, urban fiction, and horror

www.hcouturepublishing.com
Genres: beauty and fashion how-tos, general how-tos, self-help, and humor

All writers and agents please see the following Web sites for submission guidelines.

www.hcouturepublishing.com
www.0511publishing.com
www.hcoutureibooks.com

Steal my ideas section

- 24-hour babysitter
- Everything business Web site
- A how-to bookstore
- A custom clothing line for kids only
- A music therapy and ABA franchise program
- A digital virtual record company; only mp3s; everything is done with technology
- CD vending machine and burning kiosk; a million
- Become a niche publisher.
- Whatever you love
- Start a shoe line for women with a size 10–15 foot. They are out there. Seek them.
- Also start one for women with a size e3–6 inch foot. There's a need for these, too. Offer shoes at all spectrums because you created the market. Now saturate it!

I started an Internet consulting business called Steal My Ideas, Inc. when I was sixteen. I charged $250 and up for my ideas. My largest billing to date was $10,000. The business was simple. People with the desire to have their own business and the know-how to run a business but no real creativity or vision called upon me. It was like I provided the thesis and they wrote the essay.

So be my guest and steal my ideas from the list above. Or use them as a starting point to form your own million-dollar empire.

"Do today what they said could not be done yesterday and tomorrow they will be doing it, too."

"Be grateful for every mistake because it means you were given the chance to try."

"Lust a little. Love a lot."

"You must be kidding me."

"OK."

"You might get a second chance, but you will always have a first."

"The hardest thing for you is not the hardest thing on earth to do. You're blessed, so appreciate it."

"Fear? No comprenda!"

"Love what you do, teach what you know."

"There's a book in all of us."

"Are you that somebody?"

"There's no turning back now. We've come too far."

Myth 1: You are the boss

Truth: Your customer is the boss. Your role as the CEO is to listen to their needs and wants and deliver them in the best possible way.

Myth 2: You can run a business alone

Truth: If you're asking for trouble and burnout, go right ahead and try to go at it alone. Your best bet would be to start building your team as soon as possible.

Myth 3: You need other people's money in order to start a multi-million-dollar business

Truth: You might in later stages of your growth depending on how fast you are growing or want to grow. However, you should try to use what you have in order to start making a name for yourself and your business in the business world. Always remember, most investors like to invest in results, not ideas.

Web sites, books, workshops, etc.

Web sites

www.quickplans.com

www.jpatmgnt.com/jpflash.htm

www.babyphat.com

www.oprah.com

www.sweetface.com

www.legalzoom.com

www.google.com

www.sba.gov

www.vistaprint.com

www.venture-leasing.com/index.cfm?key=wcs_o-angels

www.fundingpost.com

www.prweb.com

www.beautypr.com

www.blackwealthnow.com

www.blackenterprise.com

www.blackseek.com

www.blackbusinessplanet.com

www.blackbusinessexpo.com

www.fitnyc.suny.edu

www.yourcareertraining.com/Marketing-Management-Classes.htm

www.entrepreneurshipweb.com/education/educationid/19.htm

www.latina.com

www.essence.com

www.hcouturebeautyllc.com

www.ybmillionairess.com

www.hcoutureibooks.com

www.hcouturepublishing.com

www.0511publishing.com

www.beautywaterorg.com

www.ideaanalyst.com

Books to read

Young Black Millionairess: Start a Million-Dollar Business, Volume 1 (full-length version) by Taysha S. Valez

One-Minute Millionaire by Robert G. Allen

Awaken the Giant Within by Anthony Robbins

Notes from a Friend by Anthony Robbins

Workshops

FIT (Fashion Institute of Technology) Business Enterprise CEO Certificate Program. They have great classes.

Notes and topics

These are my actual notes below, unedited. Enjoy!

- When to let an idea go (for now, not forever)!
- Get your mentality straight before starting on your journey
- You've heard it before: Nine out of ten businesses fail
- Black don't buy black
- Are you that somebody?
- 24-hour babysitting
- www.everythingbusiness.com
- Stop attacking
- My life terms
- My mantras that I believe in. List in steps.
- The deal from Random House when I get to the publishing section
- How my helper became my partner
- Contract fulfillment
- My thoughts on self-publishing
- Know your market
- Don't wait for anybody
- Go at it yourself as if your life depended on it
- Steal My Ideas section
- There are plenty of rich but not famous
- Famous but not rich
- Famous and Rich
- Do today what they said you could not do yesterday and tomorrow they will be doing it, too.
- Talk about what you can attain, what you want, and your over-the-top reach.

- Books on PR/Buzz, Business Plan, CFO, Legal Side of Business, starting a publishing company, starting a clothing company, starting a cosmetics company, opening a nail salon, opening a waxing salon, success stories, investing
- Mock business plans for each
- Business consulting firm
- If you love a lot, plan for a lot and do a lot
- Black women in beauty
- CJ Walker did it so why can't you?
- I am not knocking the hustle of music and entertainment playing devils advocate
- Why we need the sports and the entertainers, we need them to keep us out there. That is not all we need.
- What are you afraid of? Answer this question. Deal with it now before you set out to become an entrepreneur.
- If everyone becomes an entrepreneur, no one will be working for anyone. That's not true. Everyone would be hungrier. You would earn everything you work for etc. We all know we can bet the farm that that will never happen. Becoming a successful entrepreneur and staying successful is not brain surgery, but it isn't easy. I am focused on the latter of the two—staying successful. Becoming successful can happen overnight. But if you don't have the tools, you will not gain and you are more than likely to lose it all.
- The power of a great idea
- Marketing success
- Are you that somebody?
- You will when you believe.
- Money can't buy me love but it can buy me equipment, real estate, etc.
- A little bit about investments, budgeting, money management, debt reason, good debt versus bad debt.
- We're drawn to music because of the freedom.
- Music has created more millionaires—some smart, some not.
- You have to be smarter than ever to be an entertainer.

- They have clubs and books out that promote how to trap somebody with money so that you will be set for life. So make sure you mind your own business.
- Power of positive thinking
- Surrounding yourself with positive people
- OPM: other people's money.
- Invest in you.
- Read, listen, absorb, plan, take action, say thank you—so many people never say thank you. The power of a thank you is priceless.
- My cheerleader interlude. Talk about how I had no experience etc. I followed my own advice and I made the team. The next season I was captain of varsity.
- You are only as good as the best.
- Finance venture, angel , bootstrap personal, SBA loans, and grants
- Legal, accountant, consulting
- Plans: business plans, marketing plans, and strategic plans
- Millionairess: She has a net worth of over $425 million
- Don't start it if it can't go global.
- Think big or go home or stay home.
- Hot industries
- Helping others help themselves.
- Highlighting successful millionairesses in the game
- Outsource everything.
- Invest in the right team that you are tight with.
- When using family is good. When using family is bad.
- I made most of my money helping and serving.
- The new color of success
- I made my first million helping, talking, and suggesting.
- Help from family working 10 jobs
- Position yourself with the best
- The why do I care factor. Tell me why I should care? (product or service)

- Franchise
- Multilevel marketing
- Funding your niche
- Picking a million-dollar major. Talk about schools that let you build your program, etc.
- Networking
- Starting young don't try to reinvent the wheel
- Inventor licensing, intellectual property.
- List of books/audio that I used
- List of Web sites
- Look the part.
- List workshops and classes (FIT , Parsons, NYU, GIA, etc.)
- Colleges online. 2-year 4-year masters
- College vs. real life
- My note on minorities: sports and entertainment
- Blacks and Hispanics stereotypes
- Letter to my ladies
- Interview from Krystle about my future. What I am getting into
- Think like a millionaire wrap-up
- But this back in the book: Lottery style risk vs. educated risk. Or both.
- Focus
- How to succeed in super saturated markets. Give examples: fashion, music, publishing, nursing, fragrance, cosmetics, etc.
- Business research and research some more market research.com
- Building teams
- Family management
- Outsourcing
- Knowing when and how to delegate
- Knowing how to ask and seek help
- Seeking an advisor or a coach

- No matter how good Michael Jordan is, without his coaches and his team he would not be the man we know today, no rings, no championship
- Going global
- Think beyond your own culture
- Inspiration, passion, persistence, and consistency
- Taking and making educated guesses, always learning, but always willing to teach another.
- E-business: a little about that will be a full feature book. Using it to leverage your brick and moter. Or as an entity in its own.
- For e-business you must have an affiliate network and benefits, you must be affiliated with a good source.
- Inspirational quotes section
- Fear, combatting it. Just like you can convince yourself to make $50,000 a year, just add a zero. It's as easy as adding a zero. (section)
- Going global (distribution) section

Young Black Millionairess: How to Start a Million-Dollar Business (full length book), charts, graphs, the works

Young Black Millionairess: Plan to Plan, a book of plans

Young Black Millionairess: Power of PR, branding, marketing

Young Black Millionairess: Legal Basics and Not So Basics for Business

Young Black Millionairess: Success Stories

Young Black Millionairess: How to Start a Publishing House and Publish Your Niche

Young Black Millionairess: Niche Niche, from Niches to Riches

Young Black Millionairess: Investing, stocks, bonds, real estate, business

Young Black Millionairess: To Franchise or Not to Franchise—That is the Question

Upcoming division of H.Couture Publishing:
"Don't lecture me, just let me know!"
Get to the Point!™ Notes

H.Couture Publishing is calling all experts

Are you an expert at showing people how to do things in a simple, get-to-the-point kind of way? Are you an expert and success in your field? Then we need you. We are looking for experts who would love to have their works published through the "Don't lecture me, just let me know" division of H.Couture Publishing. Each book will be between 80 and 100 pages (approximately 30,000–50,000 words per manuscript). Please contact the H.Couture Publishing "Don't lecture me, just let me know" division for more details.

Areas of immediate interest:

- Fashion industry (i.e., starting a fashion line; becoming a designer; becoming a fashion writer; becoming a buyer, stylist, fashion show producer, etc.)

- Beauty industry (starting a cosmetics line, becoming a make-up artist, becoming a celebrity hair stylist, becoming a celebrity nail artist)
- Internet (surfing the Net, etc)
- Business (e-business, legal, money matters, etc.)
- Music industry (starting a label, getting signed, becoming a producer, becoming a professional engineer, graphic design for music, etc.)

I love to tell this story when someone asks, "How will I be successful if I don't have the experience?" My answer is: get the experience, train as hard as you can, and find someone who has the experience and pick their brain. When I was a cheerleader I had no idea what I was doing. I remember I needed an extra curricular for college so I decided to try out for cheerleading. I bought every book and videotape on the subject. I found the best of the best cheerleading instructor. She taught me everything she knew. I practiced some more. I tumbled, I fell, I even broke a finger, but I made it through in one piece through tryouts. I was confident, poised, and ready. I said to myself, "Give it to them like you were varsity," secretly knowing that I would settle for towel girl because of my lack of experience.

I was not flawless, but my confidence overshadowed my inexperience and my flaws. I made it through to the end and you know what? I made varsity. Not JV, but varsity. All the other girls thought I had been cheering for years before this tryout. It was the confidence, perfecting my strengths, and constantly working on my weaknesses that helped me through. Having to work that much harder and learning everything I could from the more experienced. I kept this drive with me all the way through junior year, and by senior year I was varsity all-American. That's insane! The girl who could not even do a cartwheel became varsity head cheerleader—of an all-white squad!

Never underestimate yourself. Get out of your own way. Because the only one who has the power or the strength to stop you from becoming the millionairess or heir you are is you. So keep on reading.

INTERLUDE:
Fears

Fears stop people from ever starting. What are you afraid of? Be honest. Think of the worst thing. Are you afraid of failure? I have a little secret. Failure is made up; it does not exist. The only time you can ever fail is if you don't try at all. Are you afraid of being poor, broke, hungry? How did you make it this far? You are a human being, the strongest animal of any kind. You have the power to survive anything, bear any weather. You're a lot stronger than you think. Say to yourself, "If I start this thing called business, take all the necessary steps, and it ends up not being the thing for me, I can always come back to what I am doing now (and better educated about life). But as a future millionairess, I know failure is not a part of your vocabulary. So on to the next thing. Are you afraid that other people think you're crazy, like you have delusions of grandeur? As a future millionairess, you don't need to care about the negative things people say. I know other people's doubts of your abilities don't shape what you believe in. But on a serious note, conceive making $50,000. Add a "0." It's that simple. Conceive $100,000,000. What's your number pick from year one to year twenty? My number for year one was 1.6 in the checking account. I fell a little short (1.4), but I got it. I planned, I worked, I found my team. I am fearless when it comes to trying because all I know is that I can do my best plus 20 percent more.

Bonus section

The following is an actual list of my goals for life. Each year, I revisit the list and add things or cross off things that I have accomplished. Feel free to read, and when you're done, write a list of your own. Remember, don't limit yourself.

My life goals (for now):

1. Finish my MBA in International Business
2. Form my own luxury lifestyle empire
3. Finish my demo and my press kit for my musical ventures
4. Seek management for my musical ventures (J-Pat is my preference. Only the best!)
5. Aggressively pursue investors in order to bring my company and divisions of my company to market
6. Appear on *106 and Park* and *TRL* to talk to the people
7. Get to *Oprah*
8. Launch the nonprofit, publishing, and first leg of the fashion house in 2005
9. Become a diamond grader through www.gia.edu by 2007
10. Continue to outdo myself.
11. Exercise and take care of my mind and body!
12. Shop my own reality show to show the people how much hard work goes into becoming a mogul! (My dream: VH1, MTV, or BET, in no particular order)
13. Eventually find love somewhere in my busy schedule

Your Team Checklist	Responsibilities/ Job Description	Background Experience
Accountant		
CEO		
CFO		
CIO		

Your Team Checklist	Responsibilities/ Job Description	Background Experience
VPS		
Distributors		
Lawyer		
Suppliers		

Your Team Checklist	Responsibilities/ Job Description	Background Experience
Customers		
PR director/ marketing director		
Technology Web site developer		
Other		

What do I need?

A support team:
Identify your support team (those you can go to when you want to turn your back and run). These are your home team people. They keep you going when times get tough. Keep a log of each for reference.

Business best friends:

Mentors:

Entrepreneurs group:

Industry groups:

Friends and family (a cheering crowd):

You:

Class is in session

Certificates/credentials to acquire (dates, time, cost):

Topics of interest to pursue:

Publications to read:

Web sites to visit:

Topics to Google:

Events to attend (date, time, cost):

Questions to ask everybody and anybody who is willing to help

As you start to develop your business, you'll rely on the help of others constantly. Don't be afraid to ask anything. Don't let your fear to ask questions stop you from achieving million-dollar-plus status.

1.

2.

3.

4.

5.

6.

7.

Contacts

Name:

Company:

Address:

Phone:

Fax:

E-mail:

Web address:

Notes:

Potential investors (questions and comparison charts)

Investor's name:

Contact info (email, phone, address, fax, Web site):

What type of investor (angel, venture capitalist, friends and family)?

What industries do they invest in?

What stage of companies do they invest in?

What range amount of investments do they make?

What geographic areas do they invest in?

What are their other criteria for investments?

What other companies have they invested in?

Who do I know who can help me reach this investor?

How do they prefer to be contacted?

Amount of return I am willing to give:

Any and all other questions I can think of:

My existing assets (the blueprint of my money situation)

	Clarify (amount, type, etc.)	Availability
Financial assets:		
Savings		
Income from other sources		
Spouse's income		
Credit lines		
Credit cards		
Stocks and other liquid assets		
Home equity		
Retirement funds		
IRA		
Other		
Tangible assets:		
Equipment		
Furniture		
Space location		
Other		
Professional assets:		
Marketable skills		
Specialized knowledge		
Business experience		
Certifications/ credentials		
Licenses and memberships		

	Clarify (amount, type, etc.)	Availability
Good client and customer relationships		
Other		
Personal assets:		
Education assets		
Intelligence		
Excellent communication skills		
Work habits		
Business connections		
Financial connections		
Rich relatives, friends, friends of relative's friends		
Supportive family and friends		
Ambition and passion		
Other		

Crazy ideas

Don't hold back.

Crazy ideas for marketing

Crazy ideas for sales

Crazy ideas for networking

How much money do you want to see in your checking account in year one, year five, year ten, year twenty-five, etc.? This is the fun part.

Size of my market

Estimated size of market

Is the number increasing or declining?

If either, by what amount each year?

Estimated number of competitors in my market

Is the number growing or declining?

By what amount each year?

Realistic assessment of the opportunity for additional competitors in my market

The best   Good   Moderate   Poor

The vision

What is your million-dollar business idea?

How did you come up with it?

What gets you all excited about it?

What scares you about it?

What's your purpose for starting a million-dollar-plus business? Creativity? Control? Challenge? Money?

Contact info

Send all questions and suggestions to:

E-mail: Taysha@YBMillionairess.com

H.Couture Publishing (LA Office)
468 North Camden Drive, Suite 200
Beverly Hills, California 90210
Attn: YBMillionairess

Order page for additional copies

Mail order:

H.Couture Publishing (LA Office)
468 North Camden Drive, Suite 200
Beverly Hills, California 90210
Attn: YBMillionairess
Sale price $21.00

Internet order:

Hcouturepublishing.com or YBMillionairess.com

E-book instant access order:

Hcouturepublishing.com or YBMillionairess.com

Mailing list for up and coming newsletters and books:

Sign up at YBMillionairess.com

*A*re you a
Young Black Millionairess™?

Let me know and I can write about your success. Are you an expert in a particular field? Please submit your information to:

H.Couture Publishing (LA Office)
468 North Camden Drive, Suite 200
Beverly Hills, California 90210
Attn: YBMillionairess

*G*et to the Point!™ is looking for experts in these fields:

- Digital photographer
- Great sex
- Great communications
- Motivational
- Celeb stylist
- Celeb hairstylist
- Celeb nail artist
- Beauty salon owner (starting and running a successful salon)
- Owning a bookstore
- E-business
- Self publishing
- Becoming a nanny
- Makeup artist
- Opening a boutique
- Starting a record label
- Getting into college
- Financing college
- Financing a business
- Weddings: planning on a budget

- Job hunting
- Becoming a writer
- Becoming a recording artist (getting signed)
- Opening a restaurant
- Opening a bar
- Searching the Internet
- Dieting and/or weight loss, better yet, no weight gain
- Becoming a wedding planner
- Becoming a publicist
- Becoming a fashion designer
- Becoming a celebrity lawyer
- Becoming a fashion/beauty editor
- Becoming a beauty/fashion writer
- Starting a magazine
- Mobile salon
- Personal assistant

Young Black Millionairess Series Topics

- PR
- Business plan
- Lawyer legal stuff
- Accounting
- Money
- Angels/Venture/SBA funding
- Investing in real estate
- Investing in everything but real estate: diamonds, stocks, bonds, etc.
- Success stories

OUTRO:
Think like a millionairess
(Wrap up)

- Knowing what you want and investing in you
- Go about your success as if your life depended on it
- Know that most people never become who they should be; they tend to settle for who they are because of fear, low esteem, and poor focus.
- Negativity—A millionairess's and a future millionairess's worst enemy
- You will make mistakes.
- Learn from other people's mistakes because the only mistakes you want to make are new mistakes.
- Invest in you, read, listen, absorb, plan, and take action.
- Don't start if you don't plan to finish.

Have fun and get some rest now before you start on your journey because sleep will become a luxury.

Thank you,
Taysha Valez

Printed in the United States
147240LV00002B/2/A

9 780976 768050